Someone Else to Love

DEDICATED TO JARED POLIS SCHUTZ.

Someone Else to Love

Susan Polis Schutz

Designed and Illustrated
by
Stephen Schutz

A poetic journal recording the feelings of the
author before, during and after pregnancy

Blue Mountain Press ™

Boulder, Colorado

Library of Congress Catalog Card Number: 75-37143
International Standard Book Number: 0-88396-014-1

Manufactured in the United States of America

Photos by Dan Buckner

This book is printed on fine quality, laid embossed,
80 lb. paper. This paper has been specially produced
to be acid free (neutral pH) and contains no
groundwood or unbleached pulp. It conforms with
all of the requirements of the American National
Standards Institute, Inc., so as to ensure that this book
will last and be enjoyed by future generations.

Blue Mountain Press T.M.

P.O. Box 4549, Boulder, Colorado 80306

CONTENTS

5

INTRODUCTION

The poems in SOMEONE ELSE TO LOVE
truthfully reflect my feelings before, during and
after my pregnancy. This book was
my diary; however, I changed so dramatically
during the nine months that it seems
as if parts were written by another person.

Before I was pregnant, I was not that
interested in having children or in children in
general. I associated pregnancy with
mysticism and fear; however, when I was
pregnant, fear and misery dominated
the nine months—very little mysticism. And
now, when I look at my son, I can't
remember being miserable at all. Even my
attitude on raising a child changed.
While pregnant, I interviewed nurses to take
care of our baby during the days when
we would be working. My philosophy was
that they could raise him as well as
we could. However, when it came time to
leave him with the nurses, we could
not part with him. He desperately needed our
love and presence, and we needed his.
We put a crib in our office, and Jared, Steve
and I are together, whether at work
or play, "like glue."

We are now a family of three rather than two,
interacting as three separate individuals,
in love with life and each other.

Susan Polis Schutz

BEFORE

Today I woke up
feeling strange
but special
For the first time
in my life
I thought about the fact that I
could produce a baby
Out of me
from he
a little baby
Unbelievable

Sure all my friends
have had babies
but I never thought of myself
as a man's wife
or a child's mother
I am just me, leading
my own life
and in love with he

But today, I pictured
a little baby building sand castles
and it belonged to us

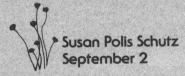

Susan Polis Schutz
September 2

11

I had a
discussion
with a group
of women
They wanted to know
why I wanted
to have children
when the world
is so overpopulated
and since I couldn't
come up with
a great answer
they thought I
shouldn't have
any
But I asked
them why they
had children
and no one had
a good reason
I thought
about this
It would be
great to see
what kind of
person would
come from
the two of us

but that
seemed too
egotistical
It would be fun
to watch and help someone
grow from a baby
to an adult
No, this wasn't
the reason either
And then all of a
sudden
I realized how
in this unstable
world
love is the only
important   thing
and most of all
a baby would be
someone else to love

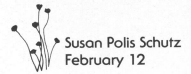
Susan Polis Schutz
February 12

When will I be ready
to have a child?
Was I ever ready for high school?
Was I ever ready for college?
Was I ever ready for my career?
Was I ever ready for anything
that happened to me?

Susan Polis Schutz
March 2

Should I have
a child
now?
It would probably
be so cute,
and it could
live in the
empty room
near ours.
But should I
have a child
now?
It will
mean months of
nausea
and interference
with my
career and
life.
It will
mean
some pain,
and then a lifetime
of sharing another
person with us.

Susan Polis Schutz
March 3

Why do I keep
putting off
having children?
Is it because
my career is
too time consuming?
Is it because
I don't want the
discomfort of
the nine months?
Is it because I fear
labor?
Is it because I
can not picture myself
as a
mother?

Susan Polis Schutz
March 10

I have never been
able to do two
important things
at once.
I am working
hard at my
writing career now.
It would be impossible
for me to concentrate
on having a child, too.

 Susan Polis Schutz
March 15

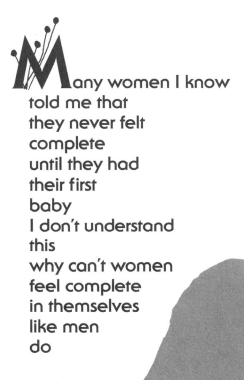

Many women I know
told me that
they never felt
complete
until they had
their first
baby
I don't understand
this
why can't women
feel complete
in themselves
like men
do

Susan Polis Schutz
April 2

I see so many women
whose lives
revolve entirely around their children
everything they do
everything they have
everything they want
everything they dream
is for their children
This is not good
for the women
nor is it good
for their children
because they all
need to develop
their own selves
with their own interests
with their own goals
with their own lives

Susan Polis Schutz
April 15

DURING

The test is positive.
It's what?
It's what?
It's what?
Me?
No, it must be wrong.
It must be wrong.
My name is
Susan Polis Schutz.
I'm a writer.
I'm not grown up enough
to have a baby.

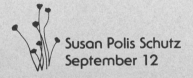 Susan Polis Schutz
September 12

23

Why do I keep crying
I'm not really depressed
Probably it's just that
I'm so very tired
In fact I'm sort of happy
especially when looking at you
but I can't seem to
stop crying

Susan Polis Schutz
September 12

How will a
child fit in
with us
We keep late
hours and
eat sporadically
We are selfish
catering only
to each other's
whims
We live with
and for each other
How will a third
person fit in

Susan Polis Schutz
September 14

Why did I take that
damn allergy pill
Had I known
I was pregnant
I would rather
have continued
to sneeze than
to take a chemical
which might hurt
my child
The allergy doctor told
me to take two
every day, and that most
medicines are safe during pregnancy
What does he
care
It's not his baby

Susan Polis Schutz
October 1

I was planning
on buying
some of the beautiful
new winter clothes
I've seen
but now
I can't
and I guess
I kind of
resent that

Susan Polis Schutz
October 2

Last time I waited
two hours to see the doctor.
Today I thought I was smart.
I called the nurse right before
my appointment to see if he was
on schedule.
The nurse said, "Yes, you're next."
I rushed to the Doctor's office
and checked in…
and waited
and waited
and waited.
I went to the desk and
told them that I was supposed
to have been next.
They said that they were sorry,
and that there were five people
in front of me.
"Your doctor is very popular
and everyone waits for him,
and they feel that he is
worth it.
He's a very important man,
you know."
"I'M AS IMPORTANT AS THE DOCTOR, AND
I WON'T WAIT FOR HIM."

Susan Polis Schutz
November 1

I can still hide the fact
that I am pregnant
from myself
because I am not that fat
As soon as I
outgrow my jeans and sweaters
I will realize that I
am pregnant
and then I'll
really be scared

Susan Polis Schutz
November 10

I can no
longer zip
up my jeans
but I refuse
to give them
up
So I now
wear my
jeans
unzippered
held together
by a diaper pin
but then I
need a very
long top
to cover
the mess

 Susan Polis Schutz
November 30

Round face
pale complexion
no waist
indigestion
exhaustion
nauseous
moody
weak
that's the new
pregnant
me

 Susan Polis Schutz
November 30

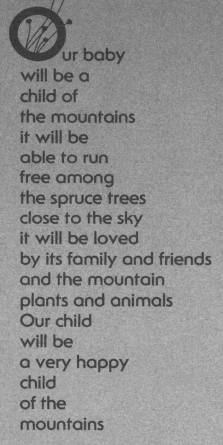

Our baby
will be a
child of
the mountains
it will be
able to run
free among
the spruce trees
close to the sky
it will be loved
by its family and friends
and the mountain
plants and animals
Our child
will be
a very happy
child
of the
mountains

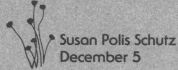 Susan Polis Schutz
December 5

Everyone keeps
asking me if I
feel the baby
moving
I don't really
know
So I get
worried
because they
say by this
time I'm supposed
to feel
life

Susan Polis Schutz
December 6

It is now
four months
I feel so
healthy
Sometimes
I get scared
because I
have absolutely
no symptoms
of pregnancy

Susan Polis Schutz
December 8

Our baby will
be very loved
by parents
who will guide it,
teach it,
and cuddle it.
But it will not
be the only
important part
of our lives.

Susan Polis Schutz
December 9

I'm very
protective
of my big
stomach
Someone bumped
into me and
I screamed
It really hurt
I know the baby
is well covered
Still it is vulnerable
and I will try hard
to keep protecting it

Susan Polis Schutz
December 10

37

We went to
NYC for a vacation—
museums, plays,
concerts, restaurants,
shopping, galleries,
bookstores;
but I didn't
have the energy
to complete a day's
activities in NYC.
I needed to nap
every three hours.
Though I tried,
it was almost
impossible to
forget that
I was pregnant.

Susan Polis Schutz
January 2

It is definitely not
fashionable to be
pregnant nowadays.
In a week in NYC,
though I saw children,
I did not see one
pregnant woman.
Where are all
the pregnant women?
Are they forced
into feeling self-conscious
because of society's
attitude toward them?
Being pregnant
is not a sickness.
It is the highest
form of being.
It is time
to honor pregnant
women rather than
force them into
seclusion.

Susan Polis Schutz
January 3

Will our baby
have sky-blue eyes
that examine
and understand
and that melt
with sensitivity
like his
father
Will our baby
get lost in
his own genius
concentrating and
deciphering
new subjects
like his
father
Will our baby
appreciate the
solitude and beauty
of the outdoors
like his
father
Will our baby
face and conquer
every challenge
becoming stronger and
wiser with each

like his
father
Will our baby
be as
truthful and
good and
honest and
gentle and
unselfish and
loving and
beautiful
as his
father

Susan Polis Schutz
January 4

I'm afraid to
feel excitement
about having a baby
because if there is
something wrong
it would be such
a traumatic disappointment
This way, I'll
try to repress my pregnancy
and then hope to be
very pleasantly
surprised

Susan Polis Schutz
January 5

Whenever anyone sees me now
they treat me as a pregnant woman
no longer a career woman
no longer sexy or attractive
just another pregnant wife
Whenever anyone speaks to me now
they speak to me as their own mothers
no longer about world affairs, nor business
nor careers, nor goals
but strictly about diapers and babies
and family life
Why can't people treat me
as the person I have always been

Susan Polis Schutz
January 6

Today I
jumped
from the
hard kick
I received
in my stomach
I wonder if an
active "kicker"
proves to
be an
active
person
If so
I like the
kicking

Susan Polis Schutz
January 19

Now I know
I have been
feeling life
It started
out
feeling
like little
tiny flutterings
almost unnoticeable
Now the movement
is much more intense
It actually
feels like
there is someone
poking me from the
inside
out

Susan Polis Schutz
January 20

People think
I have a
cold attitude
towards my
unborn child
because I
don't love
being pregnant
and because
I speak of nurses
to care for the
child when it
is born
I love my
child as all
other mothers
and fathers-to-be do
but I feel
very defensive
when people
think it's cruel
for a new mother
to have a career
of her own
and they assume
that all good women
must sit at
home 24 hours
a day watching

the baby
I feel
cold towards
these people
who criticize
me
and I can't explain
to them
that I love
my baby as
much as they
love theirs
and that my
baby will be
at least
as wonderful
as theirs

Susan Polis Schutz
February 2

No, I'm afraid
I'm not the
earth mother
that it is so
popular to be
now
I am not so
excited about
the pain of
labor and delivery
(truthfully I would
rather be knocked out
than have natural childbirth)
I am not convinced that
my baby won't be as
healthy as the
next baby because
I won't be nursing it
or because I will feed
it (heaven forbid)
commercial formula
I will use
throw away diapers,
bottles and anything
else to

make things
easier
No, I'm afraid
I'm not the
earth mother
that it is so
popular to be
now

Susan Polis Schutz
February 10

49

Somehow
I didn't
count right
I'm entering
my sixth month
of pregnancy
not my fifth
as I thought
How wonderful
to be closer
to the day
What a nice error
in arithmetic

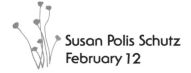

Susan Polis Schutz
February 12

I think
I have a
smart baby
inside of me.
It kicks
punctually
the minute
I lie down.
When I'm very
active, the baby is
quiet.
When Steve puts his
hand on my stomach
to feel the kicking,
it always
stops.
Already it knows
how to get
our
attention.

Susan Polis Schutz
March 8

We are not
going to buy
anything
for the
baby
or plan
anything
for the
baby
until we
meet
it

Susan Polis Schutz
April 3

Natural childbirth
the idea is nice, so are the classes
imagine—seeing the birth
of your child
I can't stand the pain though
and I really am not that athletic
Somehow I would just rather
wake up and find out
I had a baby

Susan Polis Schutz
April 6

I absolutely detest
being pregnant.
I am no longer an
independent woman
free to run
about the world.
If I honestly could
believe that there is a
real baby inside me,
I probably would not feel
so resentful about
giving up all the
physical things
I love to do.

Susan Polis Schutz
April 29

I'm getting
bigger and
bigger
My legs
hurt so much
that often
I cannot
walk
I am very
tired and
need an
enormous
amount of
sleep
but as
soon as
the baby
kicks
I forget about
everything
and can't
wait
to see
it

Susan Polis Schutz
May 3

We do everything
together like glue
We never ever separate
whether it's going to work
shopping in a supermarket
walking in the mountains
or cleaning the house
Always we are together
Will our baby be
like glue with us
Will it
be three of us
together
like glue

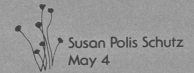

Susan Polis Schutz
May 4

What is so weird is
not knowing when
I'm going to have the baby
Each day I wake up
saying, "Is this the day
I hope not—I'm too tired"
or "I have all these appointments
today would not be so good"
or "It is so beautiful and I feel good
today would be perfect—"
but no, I'm still pregnant
I guess I have no say in
when the baby will be born—
when it's ready, it will
let me know
regardless of
whether or not I'm ready
It would be nice to have it
soon, though, so I can
return to a normal life

 Susan Polis Schutz
May 5

I am a prisoner
of my own body
My stomach is so huge
I cannot even put on my shoes
My thighs hurt so
I cannot walk
My legs cramp
I cannot stand still
The baby kicks my ribs
I cannot sit in a chair
I am so tired
I cannot finish most activities
I am so big and puffy
I hate to look at myself
My body is king
I am its helpless servant

 Susan Polis Schutz
May 7

(Four days after due date)

Lying in the
mountain sun
tired and uncomfortable
waiting
I stared at the
ground beneath me
a little two-leaf clover
peeked out under the
tall blades of buffalo grass
it looked so tiny and fragile
so helpless
the little two-leaf clover
and our little baby
I love them both

Susan Polis Schutz
May 10

61

 **"Y**es, I'm in labor now."
"Susan Polis Schutz."
"Boulder, Colorado."
"May 23."
"No."
"No."
"Yes."
"Yes."
"How many more questions?"
"No."
"Of course."
"I had measles, mumps, mononucleosis,"
"Penicillin, dust, cats"
"Can you please take me to my room? I'm
  very uncomfortable."
"Yes, I'll pay when I leave."
"Yes, I'll sign for that."
"This is absolutely ridiculous. I demand that
  I be taken to my room now. I'll answer these
  stupid questions later."
"No, I want a private room. I requested it
  this morning."
"No, I won't wait 1/2 hour down here. Are
  you crazy?"
"I'll tell you what, instead of us sitting here
  you may visit me after I have my baby. I'm
  getting the hell out of your stupid office."

 Susan Polis Schutz
May 12

Oh my God
I think I'm in labor
20 minutes apart
15 minutes apart
10 minutes apart
It's not as bad as
I thought
except that I know
it will get worse
and I can't back
out now
no one can bail me out
Oh my God
I'm really scared
This is it
no one can help me
share the pain
Oh my God
I'm really scared

Susan Polis Schutz
May 12

AFTER

A most
amazing
incredible
phenomenal
thing—
after being
in mild labor
for twelve hours,
(and it wasn't
as bad as expected)
I went to my doctor
he X-rayed me
and told me to go
home quickly to
pack my bags
I was to have
a caesarean
operation
totally unprepared
for this, I
could only cry
two hours
later, I
checked into
the hospital
those I loved
waved to me
as I was

wheeled to the
operating room
the caesarean operation
took 30 minutes
and little
Jared was
finally
here
a most
amazing
incredible
phenomenal
thing

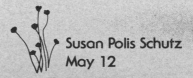

Susan Polis Schutz
May 12

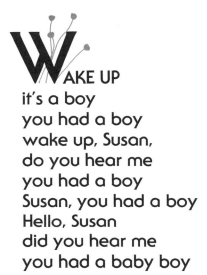

WAKE UP
it's a boy
you had a boy
wake up, Susan,
do you hear me
you had a boy
Susan, you had a boy
Hello, Susan
did you hear me
you had a baby boy

Susan Polis Schutz
May 12

Do you want to see
your baby boy now?
Do you want to see him?
No, not now thank you,
I'm too weak.
Do you want to see
your baby boy now?
Do you want to see him?
A little later, please
I'm too weak.
A little boy?
Who is he?
Did he really come from me?
Is he OK?
What does he look like?
Is he healthy?
Is he normal?
Yes, hurry, please,
let me see my
little boy.

Susan Polis Schutz
May 12

I am so afraid to hold him
He is so fragile
How do I nurse him
How do I know when
he is full
How do I burp him
How do I stop his crying
How do I diaper him
All of a sudden I am a Mother
but no one ever showed me
how to be one
I am so afraid I'll
do something wrong
Please teach me how to
care for my baby

Susan Polis Schutz
May 12

I can't believe it
I'm not pregnant anymore
it's over
it's really over
the operation is over
We have a healthy baby boy
I can't believe it
no more huge stomach
nor bloated face
I'll be able to walk again
I'll be able to play again
The pain is so
unbearable
But I don't want pills
to put me to sleep
I want to be alert enough
to realize that it's really over
it's over
Thank God

Susan Polis Schutz
May 12

Jared Polis Schutz
a whole little person
a miracle
from God
to Stephen, to me
to the world (born May 12)

Jared Polis Schutz
a beautiful little person
eight healthy pounds
delicate light skin
soft red cheeks
huge bubbly ocean-blue eyes

Jared Polis Schutz
a precious little person
who will share
our days
and nights
our life
our love

Susan Polis Schutz
May 15

If you must be in a hospital
then the maternity ward is the place to be
Everyone wheeled into it
is happier than before they came
The halls are crowded
with family and friends
The air echoes
with congratulations and
joyful phone calls all
hours of the day and night
Constantly in the background you
hear the cry of
newborn babies
The maternity ward
is really a place of love

Susan Polis Schutz
May 16

CAESAREAN SECTION

My baby was
brought into this
world without
pain or suffering.
He was born in ten minutes.
My operation was completed,
and shortly after,
I held my little son
in my arms.
What a miraculous way
to give birth
to a child.

Susan Polis Schutz
May 16

Baby
don't cry
Please
don't
cry
We
love
you
Baby
please
please
please
don't
cry
We
Love
You

Susan Polis Schutz
May 17

Jared
      a beautiful
            little son
Son
      a beautiful
            relationship
Relationship
      a beautiful
            love
Love
      a beautiful
            life

 Susan Polis Schutz
June 1

I am so tired
and weak
I have no patience
for anything
Everything annoys me—
the baby's crying
the door slamming
the stain on the rug
the scratch on the record
the pain in my stomach
everything—anything—
will I ever be
my real self again
I'm so very
weak

Susan Polis Schutz
June 2

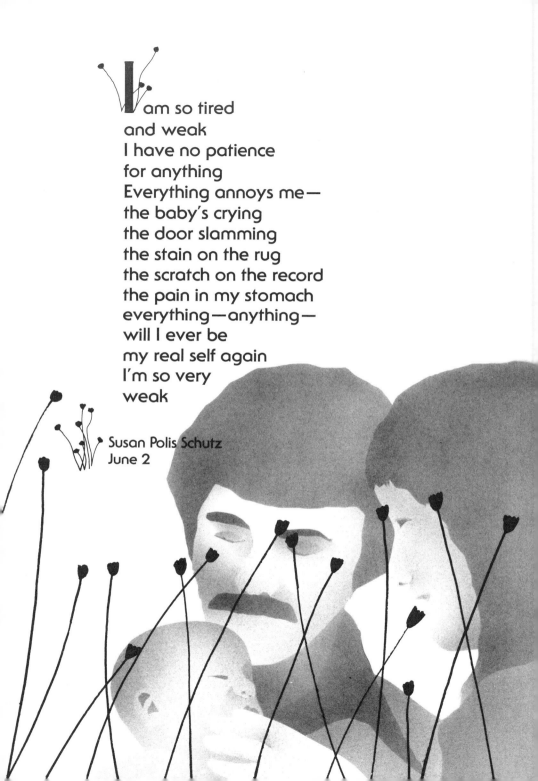

We sit here among the wildflowers
completely peaceful
overwhelmingly thankful
in total disbelief
I am no longer pregnant
We have a beautiful little son
sleeping right next to us
He too is peaceful among nature
Life is truly
a miracle

Susan Polis Schutz
June 2

Everyone: "Susan, I am so sorry
that you had to have a
caesarean."

Me: "Why are you sorry?"

Everyone: "Well, you didn't get the
chance to see Jared being born."

Me: "So what?"

Everyone: "Well, it's just so beautiful and
meaningful."

Me: "To me, the beautiful and
meaningful part is that a new life
has been born and he is from us
and will be loved by us forever."

Everyone: "Sure, that's true, but it would
have meant that much more if you
saw the actual birth of Jared."

Me: "Do you love your Mother,
Father, brother and husband?"

Everyone: "Yes."

Me: "Well, I'm so sorry."

Everyone: "Why are you sorry?"

Me: "Because you didn't see
the actual birth of them."

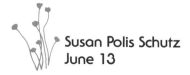

Susan Polis Schutz
June 13

Asleep in my arms
startled by a noise
he raised his little head
and looked at me
he grinned with love
as his eyelids closed
and he fell back to sleep
I grinned with love
as my eyelids closed
with
tears

Susan Polis Schutz
June 14

He cannot talk
yet we understand each other so well
I know when he wants to eat
I know when he wants to sleep
I know when he is happy
I know when he is not
When he looks at me with his piercing eyes
I know exactly how he feels
I look at him with love
and his eyes bubble
He looks at me with love
and my eyes tear
Jared cannot talk
But we understand each other so well

Susan Polis Schutz
June 14

Jared knows exactly
what he wants
he'll suck
when he's hungry
he'll kick
when he wants to move
he'll laugh
when he's happy
he'll cry when
he needs something
and no one understands
I could sit and
watch him forever

Susan Polis Schutz
June 16

I love
him so
I want to
protect him
from all
possible frustrations
He screams
because he cannot
turn over
He cries
because he cannot
crawl
He yells
because he cannot
find his thumb
He falls
because he cannot
sit up
I try to help him
do all these things
because
I love him so
but he does not

like my help
He needs to do it
all by himself
like the first time
he lifted his own head
and afterwards, grinned
at us for five minutes
I love
him so
and for this reason
I should not protect him
from all
possible frustrations

Susan Polis Schutz
July 1

85

He gives you such sincere attention
as he gives me
He treats you as a person, not a baby
as he treats me as a person, not a female
He responds to your cries and needs
as he responds to mine
He puts your demands before his
as he does with mine
He is totally honest with you
as he is with me
He loves you completely
as he does me
and we both love him dearly
for your father is everything
that is beautiful
to both
of us

Susan Polis Schutz
July 2

Little Jared
you look at
me so in need
of reassurance
I smile with
love
and you smile
back happy and
secure
I feel like I always
have to look at you
so that I don't
miss one of your
glances
leaving you all
alone in this new
world

Susan Polis Schutz
July 4

I never dreamed
how much I
could love
my little son
When we rest
in the grass
his thin arms
hold on to me
so tightly
his round floppy cheeks
rest softly
on my chest
and his tiny
red lips
lie open in
a most angelic way
I look at him
and I cannot stop
kissing him
I never dreamed
how much I
could love
my little son

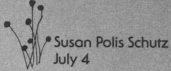
Susan Polis Schutz
July 4

"POST PARTUM BLUES"

"Post partum blues"
Surely there is such a thing
but what a misnomer
it is exhaustion
it is physical weakness
How dare people reduce
this result of a very
traumatic experience
to just the "blues"

Susan Polis Schutz
July 4

Mr. Bobbily Head
I love you
how could any
baby be so good
and so alert
and so sensitive
and so beautiful
Mr. Bobbily Head
Thank you so much
for being born

 Susan Polis Schutz
July 4

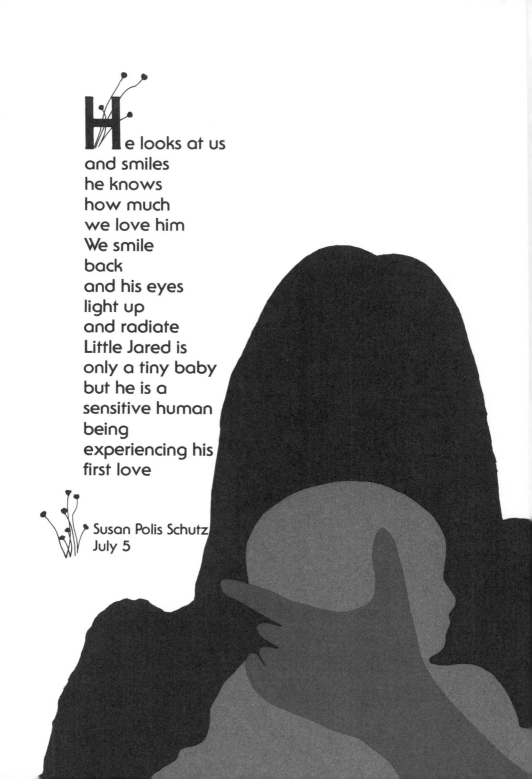

H

e looks at us
and smiles
he knows
how much
we love him
We smile
back
and his eyes
light up
and radiate
Little Jared is
only a tiny baby
but he is a
sensitive human
being
experiencing his
first love

Susan Polis Schutz
July 5

I thought
I loved you
with all
the love
I could possibly have
but now
a whole new love
    (which I never knew existed)
toward our son
has been born
and I am overwhelmed
by the emotional
warmth
beauty
and love
I share with
you and our
little son

Susan Polis Schutz
July 5

ABOUT THE AUTHORS

Susan Polis Schutz began her writing career when she was seven, producing a neighborhood newspaper in her small hometown of Peekskill, New York. As a teenager, she began writing poetry, and continued to do so as she attended and graduated from Rider College, where she majored in English and biology. Susan then entered graduate school in physiology, while teaching in Harlem and contributing freelance articles to newspapers and magazines.

Stephen Schutz, a native New Yorker, spent his early years studying drawing and lettering as a student at the High School of Music and Art in New York City. He went on to attend M.I.T., receiving his undergraduate degree in physics. During this time, he pursued his great interest in art by taking classes at the Boston Museum of Fine Art. He later entered Princeton University, earning a Ph.D. in theoretical physics.

Susan and Stephen were married in 1969 and moved to Boulder, Colorado, where Susan did freelance writing and Stephen researched solar energy. But they disliked being apart every day, and soon began searching for a lifestyle that would allow them to spend all their time together. Working together in a basement studio at their home, they created original silk-screened posters that combined Susan's expressive poetry with Stephen's sensitive illustrations of nature. With these prints, they journeyed across the United States in their pick-up truck camper, selling posters as they went. Their artistic creations and special approach to life touched a universal chord in people everywhere, and they soon had a large, enthusiastic public following. The immense demand for their works culminated in 1971 with the publication of their first book, COME INTO THE MOUNTAINS, DEAR FRIEND.

In addition to SOMEONE ELSE TO LOVE, Susan has published ten other bestselling books, with combined sales of over 10 million copies. Her poems have appeared on over 200 million greeting cards, as well as in numerous magazines and textbooks. Stephen's artwork complements all of Susan's books and those of many other well-known authors. Stephen is an accomplished photographer, and continues to study physics as a hobby. Today, the creative blending of Susan's words and Stephen's art continue to touch the hearts and lives of more than 500 million people in every country, every language, and every culture, making our world a more wonderful and caring place to live.